Spiritual Treasures

Reflective Wisdom and Prayer

❧

Michele A. Livingston

ARS METAPHYSICA

an imprint of Sunbury Press, Inc.
Mechanicsburg, PA USA

ARS METAPHYSICA

an imprint of Sunbury Press, Inc.
Mechanicsburg, PA USA

For information about special discounts for bulk purchases, please contact Sunbury Press Orders Dept. at (855) 338-8359 or orders@sunburypress.com.

To request one of our authors for speaking engagements or book signings, please contact Sunbury Press Publicity Dept. at publicity@sunburypress.com.

ISBN: 978-1-62006-260-9 (Hardcover)

Library of Congress Control Number: 2020930416

FIRST ARS METAPHYSICA EDITION: January 2020

Product of the United States of America
0 1 1 2 3 5 8 13 21 34 55

Set in Adobe Garamond
Designed by Crystal Devine
Cover by Jon R. Stroh
Cover artwork by Michele A. Livingston
Edited by Lawrence Knorr

Continue the Enlightenment!

*This book is dedicated with love to
my supportive husband, Jon Robert Stroh.
Also to my parents C. Lear and Dorothy Livingston
and to my dear departed friend, Robert J. Grant,
with respect and gratitude.*

∞

We cannot light the whole world,
But we can do our part,
For as we share our light of love,
We light another's heart.
And as each person in return
Begins to share this light,
We'll see our little flame has grown,
Beautiful and bright!

—Anonymous

Contents

Foreword

Every day I take time to pray and meditate, longing to draw closer to universal truth and wisdom. I have extensively studied the Bible and the many texts of other world religions. This research inspired me to become an interfaith minister, embracing all religions while remaining a Christian by choice. I purposely opened my mind to the words of the world's great prophets, gurus, and ascended masters, imbibing their teachings. There seemed to be a commonality, I discovered, that ran concurrent with and united all religions, regardless of beliefs, rituals, and doctrines. The truth that was acknowledged by all the great Masters was simple. *Love* is the key to soul progression: to show compassion to others, to honor our-selves and to embrace a Higher Power that is the core essence of all creation. This creates a triangle of balance, a spiritual trinity.

"The Golden Rule" in Christianity is taught to enable one to revere and respect others. "All things whatsoever men should do to you, do also to them." (Matt. 7:12) How do you want others to treat you? Be kind to them first. The concept of honoring others was mentioned and expanded in twelve world religions; among them, Hinduism, Buddhism, Islam, Judaism, Taoism, and Confucianism. For example, Buddhism states "Hurt not others in ways that you yourself find hurtful." (Udana-Varga 5,1) "Regard your neighbor's gain as your gain and your neighbor's loss as your own loss" (Tai Shang Kan Yin P'ien) is quoted in Taoism. In the Hindu religion it says, "This is the sum of duty; do naught unto others which would cause you pain if done unto you." (Mahabharata 5,1517) Islam declares, "No one of you is a believer until he desires for his brother that which he desires for himself." (Sunnah) (Reference: The Universality of the Golden Rule in the World Religions, http://www.teachingvalues.com/goldenrule.htlm)

I feel the positive nature of Christianity brings unification, and it creates self-discipline while giving followers hope that the soul is eternal. The opposite side of love seems to be the fear that is instilled in believers to follow strict rules or succumb to punishment after death. This gripping fear tends to strip away an individual's need to question his or her own spirituality and to delete the possibility of finding their own inner truth. Religions seem to segregate the masses, for many wars fought throughout history commenced in the name of religion—to dominate and convert humanity.

Contrary to this thinking, unity and love are what the ascended masters of the world taught. In Eastern philosophy, Buddha encouraged the stilling of the mind and going within to find true peace and enlightenment. It was taught that through meditation each one of us should become aware of every intention, thought and motivation to bring us closer to oneness. In the Christian religion, Jesus inspired us to activate unconditional love when He said, "He who believes in the works that I do, he will do also; and greater works than these, he will do." (John 14:12). By example, He gave us permission to be the glorious creatures that we are as sons and daughters of God – permission to love freely, heal ourselves and others, and speak our truths while retaining our own individuality in the process.

The treasures of information contained in this book were given to me through impressions while meditating. I prayed to God to allow me to tap into the flow of the mindset and wisdom of Him, the essence of spiritual reality. Jesus is the anointed one who showed us unconditional love in action—the love of God in activity.

Perceptions and interpretations came to me through hearing thought forms more than seeing visionary symbols. I do not claim to have channeled the Master but have merely received impressions from the flow of this loving energy—one of divine truth, love, healing, wisdom and creative thought. The written words contained herein are in no way responsible for reinterpreting or enhancing Biblical teachings. These inspirational thoughts were given to me to share with humanity and to enable a deeper understanding of what I believe to be the true essence of the nature of Christ.

Glean from these words what resonates with your soul, your feelings, and your beliefs. This text is given so that you may seek to become aware of universal truth. I believe that God is a powerful source of unconditional love and light. The Higher Power that created all is energy, and energy is sexless. But to keep uniformity, all references to God will be in the original masculine vernacular.

Be encouraged by these simple yet profound principles of enlightenment and know that the Creator's grace will always guide you on your soul's journey.

—*Michele A. Livingston*

Introduction

Jesus came to earth to heal, uplift, and activate the *love* within creation. Anointed by God to teach unconditional love, Jesus offered words of enlightenment to free humanity from pain and despondency. An emissary of truth, Jesus is the divine Master of life whose mission to raise the spiritual consciousness of the earth plane helps sleeping souls in darkness awaken to God's light. His transcendent nature is in every man, woman, and child. When you are kind to another, you are kind to Him. When you are hurtful to another, you are hurtful to Him. Therefore, as a messenger of light, the Master implores you to be kind, one to another.

Your soul or "light body" is the part of you that is eternal and indestructible, a part of all that exists in unity. The eternal flame in your heart should burn brightly for our Lord. The Christ was an example of enlightenment, not an example of strict and harsh principles, but of compassion intermingled with self-discipline. The *parables* are not meant to hide truths but to enable humanity to question their own principles and approach the world in a more spiritual manner.

There are many storms and rocky shores in life to weather. Take this reality in stride, for life is not about physical perfection—your soul is already perfect in the sight of the Creator. Our heavenly Father created all souls perfectly, even though some human bodies have disabilities. When newborns take their first breath, which is called the "breath of life," the soul enters the body, and the journey begins. Each soul is perfect, created by the Almighty in His image—not as a *physical* image, but as a *conceptual* one.

That which is requested or done in Christ's name will set you free from the bondage of darkness and despair. We activate miracles by tapping into the Source through belief, trust, and patience. During your lifetime it is not for you to try to be perfected, but rather spiritually awakened and self-disciplined.

God experiences everything through you; His divine creation. Be strong during the trials and tribulations in life. At times, you will encounter tests. Stand firm on the rock of conviction; hold fast to your faith and in the virtues of love and grace. God created the human soul through His divine wisdom and gentleness. Be gentle, then, with yourself and others. Understand what truly motivates your thoughts and actions—find what lies deep in your heart. "For as he thinks in his heart, so *is* he." (Prov. 23:7) Know that we all are derived from the Divine Source and will eventually return to heaven, not only to rest but to progress on our spiritual journey.

❧

CHAPTER 1

Creation

reation is the formation of all substance and the extension of the true source of love, which is God. We, as humans, are the thought-provoking *imaginings* of God; and we were *created* by those initial thought-forms. The infinite wisdom of the Higher Power sought expression, and thus a plan of divine design was implemented. Everything that exists in our universe and other dimensions was sparked from a single thought. That impulse (of thought) created energy, and that energy created form; thus, a thought produces energy, which in turn creates form. The Maker used a magnetic form of self-expression to create all, and the gift of creating our own human destinies through *thought forms* was bestowed upon us.

Every wondrous aspect of life has a rhythm. Each cell in the human body has a knowing of what it needs to do. Every atom within a molecule bears a purpose, and through divine providence, knows its purpose. This consciousness is in every animate object, much like the atmosphere and cosmos, for all is in divine order. Purity exists through the power of love and expresses perfection in all forms. Although individual human ways contain imperfections, the concept of humanity is a perfect creation in God's eyes. We have free will and the capacity to procreate, thus making us heirs to the kingdom.

Although people co-create and exist in the flow of God's energy with their own thought-forms, people can never be the one, infinite Creator. Therefore, to "honor your father, mother, sister, and brother," means, "We are all equal in the spiritual eyes of the Lord, and we are to honor our fellow humans. But first we are to revere and remain in awe of Him, whose majesty is unequaled." Therefore, give our Maker the glory, praise, and respect He deserves by appreciating all that exists.

The source of all things tangible started with a single idea, emanating from the power of the Father. Humanity refers to this creative energy in the male context by calling the Creator Father. Yet, the Creator is neither male nor female. God is a force of all-encompassing light, the epitome of wisdom and truth, and the essence of unconditional love. "For since the creation of the world, His invisible *attributes* are clearly seen, being understood by the things that are made, *even* His eternal power and Godhead, so that they are without excuse." (Rom. 1:20)

The truth of creation is universal and timeless; it will always exist on the earth plane, even though the structure of the world will take different forms. Land formations will rise from the depths of the ocean, while other landmasses will go beneath the sea. Animal and plant life will shift in appearance. The world will become warmer in certain areas while becoming much colder at the poles, where it will eventually become uninhabitable. This bespeaks of evolution.

Humans will change in appearance, as structurally, their skulls will enlarge. These changes will occur slowly and happen many thousands of years from now. The fundamental essence of all life forms remains the same, and that is the irresistible urge to procreate. Thus, the blueprint of the process of evolution is stored in each cell of the human mind and body, in each animal and marine species, in each flower and plant form, and in each changing season.

There may never be "heaven on earth," but everyone must strive to bring peace into it. Like links of a golden chain, we are all interconnected—one to another. When one can look into the inner sanctum of another's heart with kindness and look in awe at the majesty of creation, then that soul is one with God.

Prayer of Creation

*Supreme Creator, let us forever cherish and
respect all Your creation! We are in awe of the
boundless energy of this universe and what
lies beyond. We believe You love us as humans
and all creatures great and small. You have
created all things wise and wonderful. Let us
revere the fertile growth of our earth's green trees
and plants, caring for them as Your precious
handiwork. Let us look to the heavens and know
that Your wisdom lives in the vast starbelts, as
it infinitely resides in each small grain of sand.
Open our ears to hear Your profound voice
guiding and directing our footsteps. Open our
hearts to embrace all cultures and conditions
upon the earth and to honor all life forms. We
feel the rhythm of Your heartbeat on the forest
floor, see Your splendor in the power of the ocean's
waves and envelop Your tranquility in each
snowflake that gently falls. For this is the day You
have made, let us rejoice and be glad in it. As
each one of us is a link in Your chain of creation,
let us be bound together in love, understanding,
compassion, and unity. We praise You, O'
heavenly Creator. Bring peace to our hearts now
and evermore.*

Amen

— CHAPTER 2 —

✎

Love

The Lord is, indeed, your shepherd. The world He created houses His children, who are known as the "Lambs of God." He cares, and He guides. And He infinitely protects every soul. His *love* is so great that it is truly unfathomable. A mother's deep concern for her children, a man's affection for his companion dog, a spouse's intimate tenderness for their mate, or a saint's empathy for the destitute are only a minute fraction of the unconditional love the Creator possesses for His creations. This love is eternal and indestructible, without thought of self. It heals, enlightens and transcends all worldly thoughts. "Love bears all things, believes all things, hopes all things, endures all things. Love never fails." (1 Cor. 13:7-8)

This perfect kind of love performs miracles and can change the most hardened heart. The Lord truly is a powerful source of light and infinite wisdom. This creative energy force flows through everything that exists. It is rhythmic, constant, and timeless. A human soul unconsciously aspires to step into this pure flow of love. It unknowingly gravitates toward the light, as does a moth to a flame. When a soul becomes aware of the burning love of God, there is ecstasy for that soul, and nothing else exists except the blinding light of the Source.

Compassion sparks from that core emotion. So, "let us not love merely in theory or speech, but in deed and sincerity." (John 3:18) Many residing on the earth plane have not felt this higher kind of acceptance, and are therefore totally unaware that it even exists. Human souls progress closer to love with every good intention that stems from their hearts. But you must also bring back the Father's unconditional love, full circle to yourself. Each human soul is innately good in God's eyes. Even when people stray and commit heinous acts, God still loves those souls.

If your child does something seriously wrong, you should still love your child unconditionally. Yet the word "unconditional" has been overused time and again in the human condition. To love, "regardless of" what happens requires conscious effort, and forgiveness can be difficult. But you cannot love unconditionally without forgiving!

It is easy to cherish those closest to you, regardless of how they look, feel, or act. But to love those who abuse you, insult you or devise plans for attacks against you—for you to genuinely love them unconditionally—you first need to forgive them and release them to the Creator.

The inherent universal truth that lies within each soul is love. Despite this, there is crime, suffering, and abuse in the world. But this is because the earth plane is a training ground to enable humans in physical form to learn soul lessons, to choose what direction to go, and to experience the joy and tragedies of life. This world at times can be a cruel place due to its trials and tribulations, and yet it is a beautiful place because compassion through love is born here.

Humans are *wounded healers*, for all of us have been hurt in some way. These hurts promote spiritual growth. For unless you personally experience a heartbreaking situation, you cannot empathize with another's plight. You cannot open up to understand or show sympathy toward another if you have not known life's pain.

Be mindful that there is a distinct difference between selfishness and being kind and gentle with yourself. Some religions teach the masses to give to others and yet deny themselves. There is nothing wrong with giving to others if you remember to give love back to yourself. Loving your-self heals all wounds and creates miracles. Loving yourself is an act of conscious understanding through your thoughts and deeds. Loving yourself will help you to progress closer toward the goodness and purity of the Maker. Relaxation, prayer, and meditation are very important tools for learning self-love.

It was said, "do you not know that your body is the temple of the Holy Spirit *who is* in you . . .?" (1 Cor. 6:19) That means the body was created by the Source and the body houses the eternal soul. The Maker did not want to possess or constrict souls in any way; thus, each soul has free will, to be used wisely.

Anything that is done through sympathy for others, or manifests as gentleness for self, comes from God. It is *divine love* that encourages each petal of the rose to open and bloom. The mysteries of the universe are vast. Creation was not a mere accident of nature or an explosion of the cosmos; creation is a planned extension of our Maker.

In human terms on the earth plane, two polarities exist—positive and negative. The ascended masters and the Godhead know these polarities to simply be love and fear. There cannot be light without darkness or darkness without light. Humankind tends to complicate existence by overthinking it. Man has two paths to choose from: one of love or one of fear. "There is no fear in love, but perfect love casts out fear." (1 John 4:18) Decisions and actions are either love-based or fear-based. God's love protects and expands the horizons of those who acknowledge it. Fear diminishes the light and lets shadows and darkness become reality in your life. It is wise to be conscious of your thoughts and actions, and it is wise to take a clear account of your intentions on a regular basis.

The Creator does not wish you to be perfect—you are already perfect in His eyes. Human beings may feel compelled to soul progress toward perfection, for such speaks of the human condition. But your goal should instead be knowledge of your actions and motives. Becoming a saint is not necessarily what the Higher Power wishes for you. The Creator wishes happiness and exuberance for you because He is experiencing Himself through you, with your every breath, intention, and thought.

Acknowledge simplicity and give joyfully as a child. Be among the world, but not of its fear-based ways. In acknowledging love, you recognize fear. Fear is self-indulgent and negative. It produces anger, greed, and power for supremacy. Fear corrupts and diminishes the light of truth. Any dark emotion stems from fear. Yet love and fear both are needed on the earth plane for balance, for the earth plane is a training ground for experience. The two polarities must exist so that human beings can express free choice. Without the appearance of good and evil, choice is not possible. Thus, the greatest revelation of all time is the awareness of love and fear. "Beloved, let us love one another, for love is of God; and everyone who loves is born of God . . . for God is love." (1 John 4:7-8)

The race for infinite peace is not about knowledge or wisdom, nor is it about the strong or the wealthy. The true race for God's

grace and glory is simply through the heart of love. "For I am per-
suaded that neither death nor life nor angels nor principalities nor
powers, nor things present nor things to come . . . shall be able
to separate us from the love of God which is in Christ Jesus our
Lord." (Rom. 8:38-39) It is love that conquers all, transcends all,
and leads souls to their goal of becoming one with the Creator.

Prayer of Love

We know, Dear Lord, that the simplest prayers
can be the most sincere and powerful. We
acknowledge Your divine unconditional love
for us. Let us love others and the welfare of our
planet, the way You tenderly love and care for us.
In purity, with truth, kindness and compassion
let our love flow as a mighty ocean that reaches
out to many arid shores and hardened hearts.
When we touch others with a kind word,
thought, prayer, or deed, surely Your mighty hand
of love is there guiding us in the right direction.
Give us the simple faith of a child to love
unconditionally—with open hearts and minds—
all who come into our presence. We reach up in
blessed love to You, our Father, and ask You to
shield us from life's storms and rocky roads. As
our Good Shepherd, lead us in love to a safe and
trusting place where we can rest our weary heads.
Let us forgive others and release them to You. We
believe in the power of love to perform miracles,
to change lives, to move mountains of despair.
Thank You for creating us in Your image of love.

Amen.

CHAPTER 3

❦

Trust

Trust is the *utmost belief* in a Higher Power, others, and oneself. This confidence comes from faith. Faith not only comes from courage but from relinquishing control to the Almighty. Many people have "trust issues" on the earth plane, due to hurts and abuses in the past. Just as a child may get burnt physically when he or she places a hand on a hot stove, an adult may get burnt emotionally in life. But this is the way the human species learns. The child will then be more cautious about touching stoves, while the adult will be more cautious about certain close relationships. Learning to make these distinctions in life teaches discernment and engenders spiritual growth; it doesn't just promote personal protection.

Trusting means putting reliance on situations and people, knowing that assuredly God's hand is in it. Humanity is fallible, and God is perfect. Humanity is fickle, and God is ever constant with His love. Humanity remains in a learning curve, while God is all-knowing. Therefore, in relinquishing control, an individual must first put his or her trust in the Lord, and then trust in others will follow. We gain wisdom from other people and experiences while we rest in our Father's arms. "And those who know Your name will put their trust in You; for You, Lord, have not forsaken those who seek You." (Ps. 9:10)

Pure bliss is to stand in the energy of the Source—to know and to depend on the faithfulness of Him. First, trust the Creator via your faith, and in doing, you will learn to pardon and believe in mankind. There is hope for every created being, as a child of God. People create a life pattern through their thought forms and lessons learned. When you are in the stream of divine love, then every obstacle and setback seems minor. This comes about because trust resides in this *state of love*. Always trust in God. "Casting all your care upon Him, for He cares for you." (1 Pet. 5:7)

Fundamental "well-being" is created by trust. Surrender your will to the power of God. Believe in Him, knowing that He loves you and will provide for your needs. Faith instills trust and enables you to relinquish your strong-holds of control. The Creator will provide good people and opportunities to come into the lives of those who believe. "Trust in the Lord with all your heart, and lean not on your own understanding; in all your ways acknowledge Him, and He shall direct your paths." (Prov. 3:5-6)

Think of the analogy of requesting a meal in a restaurant and making a request to God. In a restaurant, you order what you desire and are served accordingly. If the meal that is served is not to your liking, you can send the meal back to the kitchen or just not partake. But to go into the restaurant's kitchen and order the staff to cook the way you want them to, or to make your own meal there would be foolish. In a similar manner, you can make a request to God through prayer, asking for what you want. If He grants your request, be grateful, for it is for your highest good. If you reject what God provides for you, it's your choice. But it's unwise when you take stringent control over aspects of your life and try to override the will of God. Request what you want, but wait and see what God provides! Therefore, it's good to ask in prayer, receive in gratitude and accept in grace.

When you surrender and trust in the Maker, He, in turn, will show you His favor. What does God request of you? He requests thankfulness, appreciation, faith, and love. Remember to laugh more and do not be afraid to love more. Be patient, and what is best for you will manifest, if you believe.

Prayer for Trust

Dear God, we look to You to give us support, like a bridge that leads to trust. Trust is as universal as faith; for together, they mean "letting go." We know You will not let us fall, for You are our Divine Safety Net. Let us remember daily to say, "Heavenly Creator, I trust You, and I totally surrender to You my mind, body, and spirit to be and live in Your perfect will. Not my will, but Thine be done." Through this affirmation we relinquish control to You, realizing that You, Father, will provide every good and perfect gift. As we believe in Your might, let our trust flow to others. We cast our worries and anxieties upon You, asking that Your heavenly angels lift us up with their wings of protection and bring us ever closer to Your blessings and peace.

Amen.

CHAPTER 4

✤

Forgiveness

To be able to *forgive* yourself and others is God's ideal grace. When you cease to feel resentment, your soul is progressing through the gift of pardon. Through God's love, we are forgiven. "For You, Lord, *are* good, and ready to forgive, and abundant in mercy to all those who call upon You." (Ps. 86:5) We are all one in the universe. Although we may feel separate from each other, we all breathe and feel emotions, regardless of our state in life. Forgiveness is pardoning by giving a bequest of love. When one is angry or vengeful against another, a negative cord is created that energetically binds the two individuals together. This is also true of the bond of love. It is greater to be bound to others by love than hate. Do not be angry with others or with God. "I myself always strive to have a conscience without offense toward God and men." (Acts 24:16)

Many have low self-esteem and cannot forgive themselves for actions that were taken in the past. Learn from your past and release it. Start by embracing yourself with love and imagine the white light of divine mercy surrounding your body. "Blessed *are* the merciful, for they shall obtain mercy." (Matt. 5:7)

Say to yourself:

> *I am a part of all that exists, and there is a blessed plan for my life. I love myself, and with God's grace I will release any anger or guilt that I have for past mistakes. All is well, and I forgive myself as I forgive others.*

After saying this affirmation, you will feel the anxiety and stress leave, knowing you are well-placed in life. You are now free from your past chains of negativity. The ability to forgive others is an act of unconditional love, while the ability to forgive yourself is an act of humility. "For if you forgive men their trespasses, your heavenly Father will also forgive you." (Matt. 6:14)

To be a pure vessel of service for yourself and others, there needs to be a clearing of strongholds such as un-forgiveness. Forgiveness does not merely mean to look the other way but to sincerely open your heart to pardon all. "And be kind to one another, tender-hearted, forgiving one another, even as God in Christ forgave you." (Eph. 4:32)

Prayer to Forgive

Heavenly Father, we ask that You grant us the grace to forgive. Give us the wisdom to forgive ourselves and the courage to forgive others. As You have pardoned our iniquities, let us try to love others as You love us. We realize everyone is human, and as human beings, we are learning many soul lessons for progression. Help us to understand that forgiveness is synonymous with love. We ask Your blessings in granting us the ability to forgive, which is the ultimate gift of pardon.

Amen

— CHAPTER 5 —

Wisdom

Jesus is the Son of God sent to educate and enlighten the world about truth. The truth is that everyone's journey starts from within. Therefore, true *wisdom* comes from the teachings emanating from various experiences, trials, and tribulations. Wisdom comes from awareness and a knowing of one's place in creation.

You were created in love by the conscious energy of the Almighty, and you are a co-creator. With your thought forms you can create your own destiny by attracting to yourself what you desire. The Higher Power contains great spiritual depth and is the source of all profound knowing. "The wisdom that is from above is first pure, then peaceable, gentle, willing to yield, full of mercy and good fruits, without partiality and without hypocrisy." (Jas. 3:17) Humanity, of course, cannot create the cosmos, yet attempts to "play God" by cloning animals and genetically altering plant life. However, humanity will never totally understand the mysteries of the universe—the perfect harmony and balance existing therein.

Soul knowledge does not accumulate immediately in life, nor do you glean it from the classroom. Life is a teacher that formulates wisdom through life's many events. It enables understanding of the self and the awareness of the motivations of the heart. From wisdom springs forth discernment, and that gift provides the ability to read the intentions of others. When someone is wise, they are in the flow of grace. "Wisdom *is* the principal thing; *therefore, get wisdom.*" (Prov. 4:7)

Consider the wise and just King Solomon. In the Old Testament, two women came to him claiming to have baby sons. One child had perished during the night. Each woman accused the other of stealing the healthy, living son and wanted him back. Solomon ordered a sword to be brought forth so that he could divide the remaining child and give a half to each woman. The rightful mother, motivated by compassion, asked the king to give the child to the other woman, instead. The other woman said to divide the baby so that neither could have him alive. Solomon tested the reactions and motives of each woman. He knew the real mother would do anything to save her child from harm. Thus, he handed the boy to his legitimate mother. King Solomon did not need a doctorate degree in psychology to employ this tactic. He looked into the human heart for the answer.

When cornered, individuals react immediately to what lies within the heart. Some people choose to deceive others through a facade. Wisdom requires being discerning, patient and prudent. It denotes long-suffering, which means waiting for guidance from above. "Do not forsake wisdom, and she will preserve you; . . . when you walk, your steps will not be hindered, and when you run, you will not stumble." (Prov. 4:6, 12)

Have trust in the divine Creator. When a decision is at hand, pray about it. Then, wait for the Father's will to manifest. He will never dictate—only guide and gently direct. Lean on Him often.

Prayer for Wisdom

Almighty God, let us be wise in all that we say and do, for true wisdom comes from You and the many experiences of our lives. Give us the gift of discernment, so that we may be knowledgeable in dealing with others and recognize who is genuine and truthful. Let us make the right decisions through patience and not impulsiveness. Teach us to think before we act and to be sincere with our actions. Father, guide us through the rocky times in life and bring us to a safe haven of peace and security. Entrust us with wisdom, so that we are capable to believe, receive, and accept what is for our highest good. Let us respect Your supreme knowledge, which created us in love, and help us to let go of our foolish pride. We trust in You, for we will seek Your wisdom with all our hearts— and there we will find it. In Christ's name.

Amen

— CHAPTER 6 —

❧

Money

Money is a tool of exchange; it is not to be hoarded or worshiped. "For the love of money is a root of all kinds of evil, for which some have strayed from the faith in their greediness . . ." (1 Tim. 6:10) Currency itself is not inherently evil. We are here to have abundant life, for as Jesus said, ". . . I have come that they may have life and that they may have *it* more abundantly." (John 10:10) So it's the intentions that lie behind the exchange of money that bear consequence.

Many people feel a lack in their lives and feel unworthy. God created all souls as equal, and each one has an opportunity for growth. One opportunity is to share money or tithe a portion to a good cause—a cause that moves your heart. No matter who or what the beneficiary is, "where your treasure is, there your heart will be also." (Matt. 6:21) Realize there is only evil in using money to manipulate or exploit others for supremacy. Love flows to all equally from the Creator, and everyone is worthy to receive. Giving is vital because it balances receiving so that the circle of exchange is complete. Therefore, apply money toward the highest advantage of all, not toward some self-serving and indulgent use or to overpower others, but as a positive means to positive ends.

Many people believe material wealth yields happiness, but this notion manifests a false god. True happiness emerges through empathy, concern, and kindness. The root of evil regarding money also reveals itself through greed, envy and the temptation to steal from others.

We inhabit the earth plane to experience abundance, but not at the expense of others. Plant your seeds of money wisely. Offer some bounty towards a cause to uplift humanity. There is no shame in material success if you share it. Be good to others. When being altruistic, you honor God, for God is generous to all. "Bring all the tithes into the storehouse that there may be food in My house, and try Me now in this, Says the Lord of hosts. If I will not open for you the windows of heaven and pour out for you such blessings that *there will* not be *room* enough to *receive it*." (Mal. 3:10)

The attitude on the earth plane at times seems to be: "The more I give, the less I will have." The opposite is true. The more you give from the heart for the right reasons, the more will be given to you. When it was said, "Give, and it will be given unto you" (Luke 6:38), it meant, "Release the thought of hoarding or accumulating money." There is nothing wrong with having security or savings. There is no shame in demonstrating monetary prudence or self-discipline. But the ebb and flow between giving and receiving require balance.

Think about how the ocean's tides essentially flow in and out; they do not stay on the shore, nor do they stay in the ocean. They cannot! Consider your money in this way. Can you keep it and hoard it? Yes, you can. But that's not the natural law of the universe. Can you give it all away and live in poverty? Yes, you can. But God wants you to have abundance, too.

The Lord did not say He wants His children to be destitute or struggling, for humanity's happiness is His happiness. But our Father provided guidelines. In possessing free will, everyone must decide which path to choose. Jesus said to his disciples, "And again I say to you, it is easier for a camel to go through the eye of a needle than for a rich man to enter the kingdom of God." (Matt. 19:24) That meant, "those who put the *love of money* before the *love of God*, denounce God." He created us, and we are His children. He is a bountiful God and wants to provide for us. So, be a living example of His principles, and then money will flow. Money is not just a tool of exchange for goods but also imbues a deeper meaning. Money allocated for higher purposes can change the world when given in love, offered from the heart, and received in gratefulness.

Prayer for Understanding Money

*Father, we thank You for the great abundance
You have given us. Let us not be driven to obtain
money for control or power, but come to You in
surrender. Help us to realize that money is just a
tool of exchange for goods and services, and that
we can use it for a higher cause to serve others.
Keep us generous, wise, and prudent regarding
our finances. Almighty God, we treasure You
first, so let money not become a false God. We
will plant our seeds of money wisely into good
soil knowing that there will be an abundant
harvest in due time. Help us not to be gripped
with fear about losing money, for You are our
Divine Provider, and Your storehouse of blessings
for us is immense. Guide us to be responsible
with our money and to always give from our
hearts. We ask this in Jesus' name.*

Amen

— CHAPTER 7 —

☙

Patience

Patience is a trait that you learn through experience. It should not be grueling to wait for something. To be patient for what is to come instills self-discipline. Without self-discipline, chaos would ensue. Patience means to bear adversity without complaining and to be steadfast in your convictions despite difficulties. In this new millennium, the heavens have sometimes noticed self-indulgence, impatience, and unruliness—a mere observation rather than judgment. So, wait upon the Lord and "delight yourself also in Him, and He shall give you the desires of your heart." (Ps. 37:4) Through trust and surrender, you can align your will with the perfect will of the Higher Power.

To learn difficult lessons and gain wisdom through experience takes restraint, a key to soul growth. "Count it all joy when you fall into various trials, knowing that the testing of your faith produces patience. But let patience have *its* perfect work, that you may be perfect and complete, lacking nothing." (Jas. 1:2-4) Patience does not mean submission or chastisement; it means to humble yourself before the majesty of a Higher Power—to wait for guidance and direction from Him. And humility does not mean self-degradation but simply honoring the Creator. "Humble yourselves in the sight of the Lord, and He will lift you up." (Jas. 4:10) As humankind realizes that they cannot create the vastness of the universe, they should remain in awe of the Source and should realize their place in the pecking order.

Patience includes leaning on your faith. Jesus in His last hours, knowing what was to come, prayed in anguish to God for help and strength. "Father, if it is Your will, take this cup (of death) away from me; nevertheless, not My will, but Yours be done." (Luke 22:42) To be obedient and patient takes courage, but if you are in the perfect will of God, your life will become more gratifying. Still your mind and listen for direction through the tools of prayer and meditation, regarding patience. Impatience resides in impulsiveness, which inevitably leads to spiritual setbacks. Impatience includes unruliness, without awareness of self-discipline.

Some may say, "He has the patience of Job." But the story of Job in the Old Testament was given as a text to show that in the greatest depths of depression and travesties of life, God's hand is always there. At first, Job challenged God's love for him, but he learned to trust and live in a joyful state through his tribulation. Thus, he was rewarded for his steadfastness.

The Almighty is in you, lives with you, and breaths through you. He gently guides you if you let Him. Therefore, "to wait" is to gain many spiritual treasures in the race of life. "Forgetting those things which are behind and reaching forward to those things which are ahead, I press toward the goal for the prize of the upward call of God." (Phil. 3:13-14) Patience is one of many virtues, but when you are aware and master patience, you are closer to the Creator's divine plan for your life.

Prayer for Patience

Our Precious Lord, You are eternally patient with us, even in our weakness and disobedience. We pray for patience to wait for Your direction. We long to hear the answers to our prayers, but understand that Your timing is not the same as ours. Give us the strength to persevere through trials and tribulations, waiting for Your grace through faith. Give us the ability to forgive ourselves as we forgive others. We believe that You can and will create miracles in our lives, if we are patient and try to remain in a joyful state. Your mighty hand is always upon us, the wings of Your angels keep us from falling, and Your gift of patience renews our spirits. We praise Your holy name, and we are grateful for all the blessings You have given to us in Christ's name.

Amen.

— CHAPTER 8 —

❧

Self-discipline

elf-discipline has numerous meanings. Primarily, it is the conscious ability to be able to pull away from substances or situations that are not for your highest good. This could be addictions to drugs, alcohol, nicotine or food. It is a difficult journey through life, and many people try to bury their pain—whether it stems from physical, emotional or psychological trauma. Pain is uncomfortable. But self-discipline yields wisdom and perfects moral character in all areas of your life.

Each earthly experience teaches individuals about themselves through knowledge of personal motives. Some people tend to be impulsive with decisions, without the thought of consequences. Therefore, it is wise to be self-disciplined and prudent—to stay in the moment and plan for the future. Some people try to run away or hide from themselves, to mask pain or feelings of inadequacy. Yet, each experience that tries or tests character is necessary for soul growth.

The temptation to overindulge comes from feeling afraid, out of control, or bored. Many times, a substance abuser cannot face life, deal with low self-esteem or handle feelings of being lost or hurt. Some substances are used to numb or erase pain. The predisposition for alcohol can be genetic, as other family members may have over-indulged, but alcohol, drugs, and other addictions can be moderated through self-control. "But also for this very reason, giving all diligence, add to your faith virtue, to virtue knowledge, to knowledge, self-control, to self-control perseverance, to perseverance godliness . . ." (2 Pet. 1:5,6) However, alcohol in moderation may not be evil, for even the prophets drank wine. And drugs can be used for the highest good for healing applications. It's the uncontrollable use of these substances that creates harm.

Temptation is also strong for people addicted to pornography; and, for those who have compulsive, repetitive, or negative ways of thinking. Uncontrolled addictions can, in their worst form, result in temptation to commit crimes.

People find comfort in habitual ways of living. Therefore, it can be most difficult to break unnecessary habits. For many, over-spending is an area where the reins need to be tightened. Money is needed for survival, but when it becomes all-consuming, it distracts you from your innate soul purpose. Therefore, if overspending is your weakness, engage in self-disciplinary practices to save money and invest wisely. Strive for a debt free life!

There needs to be a regular accounting of your intentions in all areas. To be able to moderate yourself is a great virtue, and to be aware of temptation is crucial. If you cannot immediately break away from an addiction, procrastination, or negative way of thinking, then stop and challenge it. Address the distraction, become conscious of it, and day by day, try your best to resist it.

If you need to complete a task and are not motivated to do so, then pray for enthusiasm to help instill self-discipline. Structure your time and energy to enable you to complete projects. The Creator wants you to be filled with joy and inner fulfillment, as well as to be free from the encumbrances that produce anxiety.

Perhaps you have a great talent for music, the arts, literature, or dance. If so, create time to use these gifts consistently for the glory of God. This will inspire and bring joy to you and your fellow man. Self-discipline is vital toward staying on track in all areas of life, but ultimately the creative process is one of greatness. As the Higher Power created you from His thought forms, a talented person should create with their own inspirations. To ignore these gifts is unwise. Therefore, self-discipline brings ideas to fruition and aids in the completion of creative projects. Stop for a moment and consider what you want to accomplish in your lifetime. Success comes in many forms, not only financial. What you love to do is what you were sent here to do. So, stay in tune with that career path, remain focused, and prosperity will follow!

Understanding your weaknesses is crucial for self-control. This does not mean strict, rigid tests of character; it means loving yourself enough to do what's best for you. Even Jesus was made aware of His own actions regarding self-discipline. He was a precocious child and sometimes did not follow His parents' rules. "His parents went to Jerusalem every year at the Feast of the Passover. And when He was twelve years old, they went up to Jerusalem according to the custom of the feast. When they had finished the days, as they returned, the Boy Jesus lingered behind in Jerusalem. And Joseph and His mother did not know *it*; but supposing Him to have been in the company, they went a day's journey, and sought Him among *their* relatives and acquaintances. So, when they did not find Him, they returned to Jerusalem, seeking Him. Now so it was *that* after three days they found Him in the temple, sitting in the midst of the teachers, both listening to them and asking them questions." (Luke 2:41-46)

Then, later in His life, Jesus lost His temper with the money changers in the temple and threw over their tables. "Then Jesus went into the temple and began to drive out those who bought and sold in the temple and overturned the tables of the money-changers and the seats of those who sold doves. And He would not allow anyone to carry wares through the temple. Then He taught, saying to them 'Is it not written, *My house shall be called a house of prayer for all nations*? But you have made it a *den of thieves.*" (Mark 11:15-17).

Therefore, Jesus understands humanity's struggle with self-discipline, and He commends those people who utilize self-discipline to better their lives. Know He will align Himself with those who need and ask help concerning such matters. The race for soul growth, acceptance, and perfection is not always to the driven but to the self-disciplined souls who are *aware* of their own thoughts, words, and deeds. Pray for the wisdom to know when to break away from something that no longer serves you, and for the strength and self-discipline to change it.

Prayer for Self-discipline

Dear Lord, we come to You in humility to pray for the gift of self-discipline. We are weak, but You are strong. Let us lean on You through faith, so that we can withstand the negative lures of this world that are not for our highest good. We pray for those who are hopelessly bound and chained to their addictions. Free them Father to be the glorious souls You created them to be! Give them Your Almighty Power to resist temptation and stand strong in Your light. Life should be balanced with labor, joy, laughter, and self-discipline. Therefore, help us to know that by learning to resist, we are soul progressing and growing in Your grace. We ask for perseverance to develop and use our talents wisely, and encouragement to stay on the right track. Inspire us to be the best we can be in all areas of our lives. We pray this in Jesus' name.

Amen.

— CHAPTER 9 —

❧

Temptation

Temptation means to stray from what is for your highest good, to be lured in the wrong direction. It means to lose your solid foundation of faith or purpose, to lose your spiritual strength. Temptation tests the ego through the craving of riches and power, diluting one's mission. Jesus was tempted to denounce God many times and prayed for resistance. "Therefore, take up the full armor of God, that you may be able to withstand in the evil day, and having done all, to stand firm." (Eph. 6:13)

The true temptation in the Garden of Eden was not about the dominance of woman over man or man over woman. It was not about evil winning over good. The concept of this story is about an individual who is tempted to want absolute power and wisdom to be Godlike. The thought of power entices mankind and corrupts the principles of love.

"Now the serpent was more cunning than any beast of the field which the Lord God had made. And he said to the woman, 'Has God indeed said, 'You shall not eat of every tree of the garden'?'

"And the woman said to the serpent, 'We may eat the fruit of the trees of the garden; but of the fruit of the tree which *is* in the midst of the garden, God has said, 'You shall not eat it, nor shall you touch it, lest you die.'"

"Then the serpent said to the woman, "You will not surely die. For God knows that in the day you eat of it, your eyes will be opened, and you will be like God, knowing good and evil."

"So, when the woman saw that the tree *was* good for food, that it was pleasant to the eyes, and the tree desirable to make *one* wise, she took of its fruit and ate. She also gave to her husband with her, and he ate.'" (Gen. 3:1-6)

This is the way of this world, for, on the earth-plane, you will be tried and tested—not by God, but by man and the temptations of the physical world. Humans and situations can tempt you, but God cannot tempt. "Let no one say when he is tempted, 'I am tempted by God'; for God cannot be tempted by evil, nor does He Himself tempt anyone." (Jas. 1:13) Thus, in the Lord's Prayer, when it is stated, ". . . and do not lead us not into temptation" (Matt 6:9) it should be, "let not anything or anyone lead us into temptation." So, be wary on your journey and pray for self-discipline to resist temptation.

If you feel a force is seducing you to do wrong, then stand your ground and face it, for God will not let you fall. "Therefore, let him who thinks he stands take heed lest he falls. No temptation has overtaken you except such as is common to man; but God is faithful, who will not allow you to be tempted beyond what you are able, but with the temptation will also make the way of escape, that you may be able to bear it." (1 Cor. 10:12, 13) Prayer and asking for the white light of the Creator to surround you will keep you strong. So, "Watch and pray, lest you enter into temptation." (Mark 14:38)

Prayer to Resist Temptation

*Heavenly Father, we know that You are pure
unconditional love and that anything done
through unconditional love is the ultimate
blessing. We pray that we may have the strength
of character to withstand temptation, for we
know You will not let us fall. Let us get in
touch with our own conscience, which is the
divine truth bringer. We understand right from
wrong, for it was taught to us in Your word.
Therefore, give us a greater gift of discernment,
and the knowledge to understand what path
we should choose. Give us the ability to forgive
ourselves for past mistakes. When temptation
to do wrong is strong, we know Your power to
resist is stronger! We ask for the fortitude to pull
away from the wiles of temptation and to help
others to do the same. Guide us, lead us and
direct us to a place of peace and protection.
We praise Your holy name.*

Amen.

— CHAPTER 10 —

❧

Gentleness

entleness is a spiritual strength. At times, in today's world, the value of this virtue gets trampled underfoot. With the advent of new technologies and rapid advancement, the world is a very busy place indeed. Therefore, another's needs can get lost or forgotten. Few people take the time to think about being gentle with others or even themselves! The Creator reveres gentleness, for He is gentle. "You have also given me the shield of Your salvation; Your right hand has held me up, Your gentleness has made me great." (Ps. 18:35)

To be gentle includes being patient, seeing the best in others, and lending a hand when necessary. Moderate behavior does not mean innocence or naivety. A ruler of a country can be strong and wise, yet display moderation. Think of the way a mother tenderly holds her precious newborn, how a grandmother lovingly strokes her grandchild's hair or how a husband softly holds his wife's hand. These actions demonstrate gentleness from the heart. Gentleness is a by-product of love, but gentleness has not been emphasized enough as a spiritual trait in our society.

Now think of a perfect, fragrant rose with morning dew on its petals. Imagine smelling the sweetness of the flower and touching the exquisitely smooth and fragile petals. That rose embodies gentleness when it is perceived in this way. Therefore, to instill the ability to be tender, visualize yourself as a child—amusing, energetic, and vulnerable. Honor and protect that inner child—get in touch with him or her. Go back to childhood and try to remember the good and endearing things you did for others—your happy times. Take that happiness and self-respect and focus on it. Bring the beauty of your inner child to the forefront of your mind. Feel gentleness within yourself. Let your inner being shine, ". . . rather *let it be* the hidden person of the heart, with the incorruptible *beauty* of a gentle and quiet spirit, which is very precious in the sight of God." (1 Pet. 3:4)

It takes understanding and self-discipline to be gentle with yourself. The Creator asks that you love yourselves—not in vanity or conceit, but in genuine appreciation. Though it may be easy for you to love nature, animals, and other humans, it can, at times, be difficult for you to love yourself. Yes, many people fall prey to loving others without loving themselves, so find a balance. To love God, your fellow human beings and yourself creates a *triangle of balance*. Herein is the secret of soul evolution and growth. When a soul can feel compassion for all of creation and self, then there is unity with the universe and true soul progression. Use this knowledge to strive to be gentle with all; "Let your gentleness be known to all men." (Phil. 4:5)

Prayer for Gentleness

Dear Lord, Your gentleness abounds! Let us be tenderhearted, forgiving one another as You have forgiven us. May we see gentleness in a delicate spring flower, feel gentleness in a warm summer's breeze, imbibe gentleness in autumn's colorful rustling leaves and perceive gentleness in the silence of winter's falling snow. When the world seems to turn its back on us, let us rest in the fold of Your protective grace and always feel Your gentle touch. We thank You for accepting our prayers.

Amen.

❦

CHAPTER 11

Children and the Inner Child

Children are the most precious creations in the universe! With a newly implanted soul in the body, a child is pure and still has a connection to heaven. Children are innately happy and view the world through eyes of wonder. A child loves unconditionally and uses the imagination to invent glorious worlds. Newborns and youngsters do not crave wealth, power, or fame. Children know not of these things.

Within each adult lives an inner child that is delightful, open, and innocent. Jesus said, "Let the little children come to Me, and do not forbid them; for of such is the kingdom of heaven." (Matt. 19:14) That meant you should enjoy each day, be happy, give unselfishly, create beauty, strive to love everyone, believe in possibilities and imbibe goodness.

The inner child judges not, as with prejudices, but is filled with laughter and goodwill. That beautiful part is trusting and sincere. Being childlike does not suggest being inferior, self-centered or unruly. Being childlike embraces the notion of simplicity, believing in all things good. The true way to peace is to understand yourself and retain childlike purity.

Young children give enthusiastically from the depths of their hearts, with even basic things. When adults give in the same manner, they release their inner child. Adults creating beauty in any form—through art, music, or writing—experience a similar joyfulness. The inner child believes in miracles, retains optimism, is unassuming, and adores life. So, look deep inside yourself and release your inner child.

Children exist in their own universe and create reality according to uncomplicated beliefs and thought-forms. They do not engage in analysis or manipulation; children merely explore a new and fascinating world! Children are joyful, and joy is an emotion that innately stems from the human heart. It is contagious and flows outward to others. Life demands balance in self-discipline, labor, and pleasure. Individual bliss is unique. Yes, people can revel in material things such as cars, houses, and clothing; but such feelings are fleeting. True inner bliss sustains itself through modest pleasures and beautiful things, such as appreciating a flower, a bird's song or a smile.

When in the "spirit of joy," life engenders less stress and becomes more fulfilling. Counting your blessings every day is important. Be grateful and happy with what you have, see and do; then, pleasure will spring forth and remain constant. Joy is not found in folly or idle amusements. It does not come from collecting possessions. It does not derive from control over others. Real joy is simple and comes from awareness and acceptance of gratitude. Be joyful unto the Lord, and have a merry heart! Laugh more, love more and appreciate the little things. Be attentive to all the goodness surrounding you in the darkest hours of life. Gladness begets gladness, and a lifestyle of fulfillment begins. Be yourself. Do not allow others to rob you of your well being with their negativity.

As it was written: "When I was a child, I spoke as a child, I understood as a child, I thought as a child; but when I became a man, I put away childish things. For now, we see in a mirror dimly but then face to face. Now I know in part, but then I shall know just as I also am known." (1 Cor. 13:11, 12) Although it is important to retain your inner child, this aspect of being emphasizes maturity and responsibility toward oneself and others. All humans advance from being innocent to being (hopefully) wise and responsible.

Appreciate all the seasons of your life. Spring is like the new baby, fresh and filled with hope. Summer is youth, filled with promise and bounty. Autumn is the prime of life, filled with colorful experiences, the ability to release the past like falling leaves and prepare for the future. Winter is the time of reflection, stillness, and sleep. It's the time of the end of one's mortal life. Do not mourn if a loved one's time has ended in spring (infancy), summer (youth), autumn (prime) or winter (old age). "To everything there is a season, a time for every purpose under heaven:" (Eccl. 3:1) Elderly people tend to reminisce about their childhoods or sometimes behave in a child-like way. This happens because their time of transition is nearing for crossing over. Before they enter the kingdom of heaven, a total perspective of life with new insights emerges.

But, you must remember to look within yourself daily and acknowledge that special, inner child. Embrace and love this child. Let the child in you out to play. This elementary task opens the true path to happiness and the soul's enlightenment!

Prayer for Children and the Inner Child

Dear Father, we come to You to ask Your blessings for our precious children, for Jesus said not to rebuke them, but welcomed them with love into His open arms. Let us all be as little children— loving, laughing, trusting, and believing in Your grace. Yes, we are all Your children, in the fold of Your goodness and protection. Let not the innocent ones suffer in any way this day. We pray for Your holy angels to intervene and watch over these little ones. Shower us with Your mercy and let us teach our children what is good and wise. We are all Your "lambs." And You, Dear Lord, are our Shepherd, who guides and leads us to a better, safer place. Bless those children now who seek love, but cannot find it, who seek protection where there is none. Let these cherished ones suffer not, but be comforted in Your arms this very moment! Help us all to release our "inner child" with enthusiasm and joy; for the child within believes in miracles, is filled with wonder and trusts in You. Thank You for hearing this prayer, given in love.

Amen

— CHAPTER 12 —

❧

Pets and the Animal Kingdom

The Lord created the *animal kingdom*, not to serve human beings, but to coexist with them. Every living, breathing creation has a purpose. Water is filled with living organisms, and it is one of the elements vital for the continued existence of plants, animals, and people.

Knowledge is key in interacting with the animal population. All animals are sentient beings—whether they are on the land, in the air or in the sea. God protects all His creatures, "look at the birds of the air, for they neither sow nor reap nor gather into barns; yet your heavenly Father feeds them." (Matt. 6:26) Animals are intuitive, emotional, and intelligent. Conversely, they have memories. Animals experience love, despair, and joy. So, with that, do not treat them as beneath you. "For every creature of God *is* good, and nothing is to be refused if it is received with thanksgiving." (1 Tim. 4:4)

In having a pet, a bond forms for eternity. This is a bond of energy called devotion that can never be broken. If a pet's caretaker passes to Heaven first, the pet may experience loneliness and confusion. If pets are carelessly given away or left behind, they may feel abandonment and sadness. Emotional scars may develop, especially when a pet feels unwanted or neglected. If animals encounter mistreatment, they experience anxiety, not only through physical abuse but even mental anguish from being talked to in an unkind way.

Humanity should respect all creatures, great and small, in all kingdoms of the world. At times, humanity uses animals in cruel ways, such as beasts of burden or for laboratory testing. But awareness of animal welfare and their true being as sensitive and telepathic creatures is expanding. The Lord watches over both man and beast. For it was written, "Your righteousness is like the great mountains; Your judgments *are* a great deep; O Lord, You preserve both man and beast." (Ps. 36:6)

A caretaker of animals needs to treat these blessed creatures with compassion and respect, and not as disposable commodities. Every pet is a responsibility, not to be neglected when no longer convenient or useful.

When a person befriends and loves a pet, the *spirit* of that animal and the *soul* of its caretaker may bond and form a *soul group* in Heaven. The essence of the beloved pet will wait for you if it passes away first. Energy cannot be destroyed—it just takes another form. Therefore, the *energy* of a sentient animal is eternal and indestructible, just as with human souls.

Pets are here to teach us unconditional love—how to give it, how to receive it. They are as helpless as children and depend upon us for sustenance and care. They empathically feel our emotions.

Pets can even absorb negative vibrations around their caretakers to help alleviate their human friend's emotional pain.

If you are cruel to animals, a spiral of dark energy may develop around you, for what we give out comes back to us! This statement is said in truth and observation.

It is a reality that humankind must nourish the body, and animals have been provided for food and sustenance for many eons. This meets with approval. However, the animals should be treated humanely while living and not put to a torturous death. No animal should ever be tortured! For, "a righteous *man* regards the life of his animal, but the tender mercies of the wicked towards them are cruel." (Prov. 12:10)

With today's technological advancements, animal experimentation is no longer necessary. Fortunately, a global mass shift in consciousness is altering our treatment of animals. When people hurt them, this transgression weakens the link of love throughout the world. Our earthly realm is a training ground, and the most important lesson is showing sympathy to all of creation—*including* the animal kingdom!

If you do not wish to have a pet or be a caretaker of animals, that's fine with the Creator. If you kill an animal in self-defense, it will also be pardoned. But when pre-meditated abuse occurs against an innocent creature in the animal kingdom, it will not be overlooked—especially during your *life review* process following death. Therefore, be loving, respectful, and caring of animals as a mother would for her children; and learn from this truth.

Prayer for Pets and Animals

Protect our precious pets Dear Lord and all the animals of the world. For we know that the animal kingdom is a part of Your wonderful creation! Help us to realize that animals are sentient and empathic beings that need compassion, love, and protection. Let each animal that gives his or her life for our nourishment be humanely treated. As co-inhabitors of our world, may we respect all creatures, great and small. We appreciate the unconditional love we receive from our pets, knowing that they are like our family members. Watch over the animal populace—those in the air, on land and sea—and let us be concerned for their welfare. We have it within our grasp to preserve animal populations that may soon become extinct. Let us be encouraged to do our part. Give us the power to do what is right for our pets and animals, for we know that love never dies and that they will share a place with us in eternity.

Amen.

CHAPTER 13

❧

Faith

What is *faith*? Faith is a virtue that steadfastly perseveres through all obstacles in your life. Faith is the divine light that pushes through the darkness; it is a belief that all will be well when there is no immediate proof. It's a *knowing* in your soul that what is meant to be will be! This belief is an energy of determination and trusting God, knowing that He will bestow upon you what is for your highest good. Faith is an indomitable strength in mind, body, and spirit to overcome stumbling blocks and move mountains of despair. "Now faith is the substance of things hoped for, the evidence of things not seen." (Heb. 11:1). Put your confidence in the Creator; align your will with His. In the New Testament a woman had been hemorrhaging blood for twelve years. She knew in her spirit that if she just touched the robe of Jesus, she would be healed. When she touched His hem, Jesus turned and said to her, "Be of good cheer, daughter, your faith has made you well." (Matt. 9:22)

Faith is a springboard for miracles. It is difficult to trust in the unseen and keep your faith, but faith has its rewards. We are watched over by the Lord and staunchly protected, no matter how far down we fall. "If we are faithless, He remains faithful; He cannot deny Himself." (2 Tim. 2:13).

The air is invisible, and yet we need oxygen to live; the electromagnetic field surrounding our body is invisible, and yet Kirlian photography has captured this energy. Love cannot be seen but only felt by the heart. Therefore, "we walk by faith, not by sight." (2 Cor. 5:7). Believe in the loyalty of the Almighty. Open your mind to possibilities and keep your dreams alive. Prayer is the catalyst of allegiance to your faith. To embrace this concept is a crucial lesson many are here to learn. By releasing control to God, you are "looking unto Jesus, the author, and finisher of *our* faith." (Heb. 12:2)

Prayer for Faith

*We are aware, Father, that we walk by faith
and not by sight when we believe in Your word.
Through the power of Your Spirit, let the gift
of faith enter our hearts. Give us the fortitude
to keep moving forward on our path through
emotional roadblocks, for we understand that
faith is the substance of things that we hope for,
and faith is the evidence of things to come—
which are now unseen. When we feel low, in the
pit of despair, let the hand of faith reach down
and gently lift us up toward Your light. Give
us the character to be strong in trials, patient
through tribulation, and staunchly trust in Your
ever-constant love and grace.
We pray in Jesus name,*

Amen.

— CHAPTER 14 —

❧

Hope

At times humanity seems to be held in the grip of despondency and despair without *hope*. We search for answers to life's deepest questions, which cannot always be answered. The longing to know if the soul is eternal and what occurs after death perplexes many. Faith must be encouraged to dispel anxiety. A very important component of faith is hope, which tends to squelch the depression many feel. Therefore, faith and hope reside together.

Hope brings peace for you to believe that the outcome of life will be good. You need this belief the most when you have an urgent need to be met, and hope puts a reassuring slant on the future. Hope is for the next moment, the next day or the next year. To desire in your heart means to lean on the Higher Power through faith, knowing you are provided for and protected. "Now, hope does not disappoint, because the love of God has been poured out in our hearts by the Holy Spirit who was given to us." (Rom. 5:5)

There is power with this reliance because it comforts, encourages, and uplifts humankind. You are receiving a positive flow of energy from your thought forms when you retain this attitude. It is beneficial to first count your blessings and then ponder the wonderful things the Creator has given to you daily.

In the bleakest of times, life is not easy. But we are here to learn life lessons and grow spiritually. Hope banishes negativity and lets sunshine into every small, darkened crevice of the mind; it enlightens the heart and renews tranquility.

Belief in humanity's goodness and the Father's grace instills hope for the future. You should speak words of hope, give positive affirmations, and communicate love. Yes, speak good things—make inspired, confident statements to yourself and others and let God's love speak through you. "Every word of God *is* pure; He *is* a shield to those who put their trust in Him." (Prov. 30:5)

Spiritual nourishment (not just physical nourishment) is important for change to occur. Self-discipline, communing with God, and giving to others bears fruit—one positive emotion begets another as one transcendent thought alleviates fear. Hope casts out fear because it stems from love. There is no room for love and fear to reside together. Worry and desperation are born from the fear of loss. Therefore, to overcome these emotions, you must make a conscious effort to replace fear with love to create hope for inner peace. We should ". . . rejoice in the hope of the glory of God. And not only *that*, but we also glory in tribulations, knowing that tribulation produces perseverance; and perseverance, character; and character, hope." (Rom. 5:2-4)

Expectation brings sunshine with a new dawning—a new beginning. Pray for the power of expectation. Regarding hope, God's timing is not necessarily the same as our timing. His thoughts are higher than our thoughts. Therefore, strive to be patient and step into the stream of hope through faith and prayer. The Creator's wish for every human being is to be happy, to co-create with love, and to give consideration to others. When love resides in the human heart, so does hope. "For we were saved in hope, but hope that is seen is not hope; for why does one still hope for what he sees? But if we hope for what we do not see, we eagerly wait for it with perseverance." (Rom. 8:24, 25) Hope is one of the greatest gifts that we can give to one another and to ourselves.

Prayer for Hope

*Heavenly Creator, we pray that Your Holy Spirit
descends upon us, like a gentle dove of hope.
When we stand alone, let us feel Your presence
enfold us, and Your light protects us. And like
a lighthouse, in the darkest of times, let us be a
beacon of light to spread hope to others. Each
new day is a new beginning that gives birth to
hope. We pray to persevere through setbacks and
to look with expectation for a better tomorrow.
We pray this in Christ's name,*

Amen.

— CHAPTER 15 —

❧

Peace

Peace is quiet tranquility, restfulness, and calmness. It represents a repose through freedom from war, violence or dissension. With all the chaos and unrest surrounding us in this world, it is sometimes difficult to feel grounded and balanced. Peace is not the absence of power, but the presence of love. Strive for peace in your hearts and be aware of taking time to love yourself, which results in delivery from anxiety. Peace instills order and security, not only in your own life but those around you. "Therefore, let us pursue the things which make for peace and the things by which one may edify another." (Rom 14:19) If you are depressed, you could be dwelling in the past. If you are anxious, you may be worrying about the future. "Therefore, do not worry about tomorrow, for tomorrow will take care of itself."

(Matt. 6:34) To be in peace means to live in the moment. Faith is also a component of peace. If you feel unrest, have a compulsion to worry or feel extremely vulnerable; pray that your faith will instill peace within.

It was Jesus, the Master Teacher, who brought faith through peace to His disciples when He decided to travel to the other side of the waters to teach. Jesus wanted to reach as many people as possible. A major portion of His ministry took place around the shores of the Sea of Galilee, an area widely influenced by the Romans and the Greeks. It was at the eastern shores of the sea where cities were very diverse culturally, religiously, and geographically from the major Jewish cities located on the waters' western shores. Jesus concentrated His teachings and miracles in these western Jewish towns. This population was known as "our side." But Jesus sometimes traveled to the "other side" to teach the people known as the Eastern Gentile region.

One evening He said to His disciples, "Let us cross over to the other side." They had just left another multitude, and they took Him along in the boat as He was. And other little boats were also with Him. And suddenly a great storm arose, and the waves beat into the boat so that it was already filling. But Jesus was in the stern, asleep on a cushion. And they awoke Him and said to Him, "Teacher, do you not care that we are perishing?" Then He arose and rebuked the wind and said to the sea, "Peace, be still!" And the wind ceased, and there was a great calm. But He said to them, "Why are you so fearful? How is it that you have no faith?" (Mark 4:30—40). So, when fear overcomes you, remember that Jesus is not asleep. Pray for the faith to have peace in the moment to overcome fear. For He is the Prince of Peace! Worry is a natural human emotion, and when you are worried it's because you may be trying to do everything yourself; when you're at peace, you surrender and remember that God is in control. Lean on the Spirit of

God and take your troubles to Him through prayer. Remember, ". . . to be spiritually minded is life and peace." (Rom. 8:6) Seek God's counsel first, for He will never drop you or forsake you. You will be granted peace, which pleases the Almighty. "The Lord will give strength to His people; He will bless His people with peace." (Ps 29:11) Peace is for everyone, so pray for others to have peace in their hearts as well. "If it be possible, live peaceably with all men." (Rom. 12:18)

Sharing peace is still evident in the Middle East. Even today, the common greeting, "Peace be with you," and "Peace be with you also," is exchanged among friends. If a fight or disagreement occurs between friends, a person may ask for his peace back! The other person returns peace with the phrase, "I give your peace back to you."

Thus, it takes awareness, perseverance, and gentleness with self to feel peace within. And when there are times of anxiety, when you falter, remember one of the most profound messages Jesus ever gave us: "Peace I leave with you. My peace I give unto you; not as the world gives do I give to you. Let not your heart be troubled, neither let it be afraid." (John 14:27) Peace is the inner knowledge that your relationship with God is secure.

Peace be still!

Prayer for Peace

Dear Lord, please instill peace within us. Let our thoughts, intentions, motivations, and spirits remain calm. Help us to have the faith to know that peace will remain in us and that peace will surround and enfold us like the wings of angels! As a gentle waterfall, let peace flow through us and wash away any doubt, fear, negativity, or anxiety. We are now in the arms of perfect peace, and our hearts are engulfed in its serenity. Thank you for your many blessings.

Amen.

CHAPTER 16

❦

Protection

The world can be a very chaotic place, and we as humans may feel vulnerable, restless, and at times, out of control. *Protection* means there is guardianship over an individual, a barrier, a buffer, and a divine shield against any form of danger. The Master Christ knew that God is the ultimate protector of our insecurities, our suffering, and pending harm that may occur. Some may question why their life is so difficult. It may seem like there is one failure or test after another and no protection against adversity. There needs to be a belief that the Creator contains great power and has the consummate ability to oversee and protect us when necessary. "For He shall give His angels charge over you, to keep you in all your ways. In their hands they shall lift you up, lest you dash your foot against a stone." (Ps. 91:11, 12) We all have an angel assigned to us at birth to be our guardian, as well. Angels have never inhabited a human body. They are "light beings" created by God to defend, safeguard, and shelter us, so even when we feel alone, we are never truly alone.

Many times, the Christ and God Himself have been alluded to, as the "Good Shepherd," who watches over us, finds us when we are lost and guards our well being. "The Lord is my shepherd; I shall not want. He makes me to lie down in green pastures; He leads me beside the still waters. He restores my soul; He leads me in the paths of righteousness for His namesake." (Ps. 23:1-3)

Jesus told the Pharisees who opposed Him and accused Him of interacting with the tax collectors and so-called "low lifes" of the time, a simple shepherd's parable! The story indicated that even those who are lost are still protected and found. "For the Son of Man has come to save that which was lost. What do you think? If a man has a hundred sheep, and one of them goes astray, does he not leave the ninety-nine and go to the mountain to seek the one who is straying?" (Matt. 18:11, 12) Then and now it is almost a daily occurrence in a shepherd's life to look for a sheep that has strayed from the flock. The shepherd's job is to protect and oversee the whole flock. Even today, in the Judean wilderness, a shepherd will appoint other shepherds to watch his flock while he goes to find one lost sheep. In the twisted folds and narrow canyon gullies of the wilderness, it is easy for a sheep to stray into the open mouth of a cave or wander aimlessly down a riverbed. The shepherd will search and call out for the lost one. Once he has found his lamb, he places the lamb tightly around his shoulders for safety and rejoices that his sheep is found.

Jesus' story, told to the Pharisees, indicates that God is constantly guarding, protecting, and caring for all of us, regardless of social status. Then let us also look to the Christ, the Good Shepherd, keeping our eye on Him for safety, security, and guidance.

Prayer of Protection

Heavenly Father, help us to feel secure and protected this day. We are in Your flock as Your "Lambs of God." When we are lost, and the trials of life push us into rocky, dark, and lonely places, let us feel Your divine power overseeing us, protecting us, and leading us home into Your mighty arms of safety. We understand that life isn't an easy journey, but in truth let us remember that there is no power greater, more loving, and more shielding than Yours. We thank You for your many graces and blessings in Christ's name.

Amen.

— CHAPTER 17 —

❧

Religion

Each world *religion* believes it defines the best way to serve. The great ascended masters and teachers did not speak of separate religions or belief systems; they spoke of truth, unconditional love, and spiritual reality. Many prophets have been born throughout time in each civilization of the world. They have all preached and taught similar concepts—to let love flow throughout the universe with your upright thinking, to do unto others as you would have them do unto you, and to honor the Creator while remembering we are all one.

In Christianity, doing unto others as you would have them do unto you is called the *Golden Rule*. "Therefore, whatever you want men to do to you, do also to them." (Matt. 7:12) From the teachings of these enlightened masters, religions have been founded. But humankind has sometimes formed strict parameters on these belief systems, incorporating their own rituals and dogmas that at times force others to believe in principles that may be confining and fear-based.

The anointed ones who brought God's truth to the earth did not necessarily wish to have religions created from their teachings. These ascended souls merely chose to incarnate to teach and set examples of love and healing. One religion is not better or greater than another, for the base element is simply to *love*. The strict guidelines set upon the masses are humanly devised, not God-rendered. Each individual soul whom the Lord created has a unique mind, personality, and memory bank. Each person must learn soul lessons while on the earth plane. Religion generally provides helpful guidelines that keep people unified, hopeful and self-disciplined. Conversely, religion teaches tradition and the difference between right and wrong, which is also good. But the *true* essence of our time here on earth is about finding God through direct communication with Him in our own distinct way, without dictation.

According to the *New Testament*, Jesus rejected certain ritualistic beliefs of the Jewish church and preferred to be alone to communicate directly with the Father. "But you, when you pray, go into your room, and when you have shut your door, pray to your Father who *is* in the secret *place*; and your Father who sees in secret will reward you openly." (Matt. 6:6)

Difficulty arises in an ego-based world, where men are in opposition to women; religions and politics clash ardently with themselves and each other, and race wars and fights for supremacy emerge. Tolerance and equality are vital keys for obtaining moral thinking and peace. Humankind, at times, is not aware of the underlying unification—the oneness that permeates all. We sometimes fall short of remembering that we all have a place as God's children, regardless of our economic status, religious beliefs, race designations or political orientations.

— Religion —

Prayer of Religion

Dear Lord, we come to You from different religious backgrounds, beliefs, systems, and traditions. In Your divine wisdom, You have created each one of us in Your image—one of love—to inhabit this world. Therefore, let us, in turn, love one another, as You love us, without judgment or hypocrisy. Let us truly know You and serve You in our own distinct ways. No matter what our religious affiliation, let love, forgiveness, and compassion be our foundation.

Help us try not to fight over who we think is right or wrong, or dictate what we feel is the best way to serve. Remove any shackles of intolerance, pettiness or prejudice from our spiritual eyes.

Help us to clearly see the true essence of Your word, which is love. Dear Lord, if it is Your will, let our hearts lead us to the appropriate religious teachings, where we will find lasting peace; and there, may we greater share our time, gifts and talents to glorify Your name.

Amen.

— CHAPTER 18 —

∝∞

Spirituality

Spirituality differs from religion; you can be spiritual but not necessarily religious. Although religion fosters certain needed control of the masses and keeps a semblance of social order, there have been many wars fought on the earth plane in the name of religions. Our Creator is not about war or dominance. He wants His children to have abundance, to be fruitful and giving, one to another—and not be dictatorial. When a person is spiritual (filled with the spirit of God), then there is no room for condemnation, only love. A spiritual person is seeking to find answers in their own way through love, regardless of what others believe. They keep an open frame of mind with an attitude of compassion. Therefore, do not allow others to dictate your beliefs and actions.

Go directly to the Source through prayer and meditation, communicate with God, and you will find spiritual fidelity and ultimate peace. Find your own unique spark, that which you have to offer, and give it to humanity with joy. You are an extension of all that is good, created in love to seek and to serve.

Think of a large oak tree in autumn. Every leaf that falls from the tree has served the tree; one leaf is not better than another, for all are equal. The tree is like God, the foundation of whose roots are strong. The leaves are as humans and are an extension of that foundation. When the leaves have served their purpose, it is time for their "season of rest"—to die—and then be reborn in the spring. This is the cycle of living—birth, growth, abundance, rest, and death—and then the cycle begins again. The leaves are part of the whole tree—each one different, yet unified. Humanity is part of the "tree of life"—serving as the foundation of the world. Everything is woven and interconnected.

Therefore, "Let not your heart be troubled;"(John 14:1) Pray that the Creator will reveal himself to you in a way that is right for your soul's growth. "That your faith should not stand in the wisdom of man, but in the power of God." (1 Cor. 2:5) Seek a higher road, a greater personal calling, and all will be well.

Prayer of Spirituality

Heavenly Creator, let each one of us seek You and find You in our own way, in a way that pleases You. We long to commune with Your unconditional love, long to help others, and bring unity to this world. We are all spiritual beings enveloped in Your spirit of grace. Let us feel Your Holy Spirit within us, gently guiding and directing us to the right path. Whether we find peace in a religious place of worship or on a spiritual walk in nature, it is You who we revere and praise. Let our beliefs keep us open to all Your children, without condemnation or constraint. Keep us from dictating to others what they should do, know or believe. Love and understanding is the universal language for all that exists. We thank You for giving us free choice and will and pray that what we do is pleasing in Your sight.

Amen.

— CHAPTER 19 —

꧁

Soul Purpose

Since the earth plane is a training ground for soul advancement, we are here to work in unison to help raise the spiritual consciousness of humanity. Consciousness means "awareness." Although many are *aware* of good and evil, love, and fear, they do not know how to resist the temptation to serve themselves. Being gentle with yourself is different than being selfish. Because of free will, humanity sometimes gravitates toward serving self, and that is their choice.

In this new millennium, there are many lightworkers on the earth plane who are trying to awaken the sleeping masses (the spiritually unaware). Jesus came to teach us about compassion, and to share the idea that what motivates the heart motivates the human being. Souls who have had various life experiences and learned from them tend to be more discerning, wise and patient. They are sometimes referred to as "old souls." Souls who have not had as many in-depth growth experiences may unconsciously tend to be prideful and self-indulgent, for they are still learning many soul lessons. These souls are sometimes referred to as "young souls." Souls choosing positions of leadership are not necessarily older souls. Nor must a soul be in an authoritarian position to progress. No matter what stage of evolution souls are in, all are equal and perfect in God's eyes because all were created through love.

Your *soul purpose* lies in what your soul agreed to accomplish before your birth. How do you feel about your life, career, and skills? Do you love your work and derive great satisfaction from helping others through your special gifts and talents? Many people just "go through the motions" of having a job to merely earn an income. The career you chose should coincide with what you love to do and what stirs your inner being. Some people feel trapped in a fruitless job, thinking they lack the necessary skills to do otherwise. Self-confidence issues may hinder you from stepping out to try something new. Through meditation, be aware of two motivational factors—what you love to do and where your innate skills lie. This will lead you to your soul purpose for this lifetime. When you are engaged in what your soul is here to accomplish, and it agrees with the perfect will of God, your work will be joyful! "Be steadfast, immovable, always abounding in the work of the Lord, knowing that your labor is not in vain in the Lord." (1 Cor. 15:58)

The physical world (in humanity's eyes) is imperfect—some people have mental aberrations, delusions, or physical disabilities, while others are in dire poverty and starvation. These events are not random situations inflicted on humans by an omnipotent God. These situations occur because we unconsciously choose them as a pre-birth measure (meaning our pre-existing soul chooses these conditions for spiritual growth on the earth plane).

As previously stated, your soul is eternal. Your soul is a spark from the divine flame of the Creator. You then can co-create. For as Jesus said, "Most assuredly, he who believes in Me, the works that I do he will do also; and greater *works* than these he will do." (John 14:12) Your thoughts create your reality, whether your thoughts flow in a positive or negative way.

Throughout the history of the earth plane, all ascended masters of the light have come here to set an example of mastery over fear and the dark polarity. To help enlighten humanity and make the world a better place, souls choose a life theme before birth. Souls bring certain talents with them when they incarnate into the physical body, but these talents can be further enhanced through experience and dedication. Some souls are here to serve and heal humanity. Some souls choose to be innovators in science, art, or technology, while still others choose to take up causes, such as conservation or global changes.

Do not belabor the past. Learn from it. Every thought and action is a soul experience and is recorded in your *record of life*. The Creator knows and sees all in infinite wisdom. The crux of your journey is not about fame, wealth, or recognition; although there is nothing wrong with these conditions, your purpose should be to learn important lessons and enrich the lives of others. As was said, the true purpose of life is to know and respect yourself, love and care for others and serve the Higher Power.

No one soul is better than another, but some souls choose to experience more trials and tribulations to enhance their spiritual growth. It is wise to view yourself as a self-empowered being who can do anything, including performing miracles! "I can do all things through Christ who strengthens me." (Phil 4:13)

Confusion may linger concerning what life purposes are at hand because a form of amnesia occurs when your soul enters your body at birth. Your challenge is to realize your life theme and then try to accomplish it. What is the best way to progress? It is an individual choice.

Serving is not better than creating, nor is creating better than healing. Everything is one. Knowledge of self-empowerment is necessary for growth but not as a goal for supremacy. Souls are on an infinite evolutionary journey. What your soul does in a lifetime guides the physical body to accomplish the mission it has chosen. If you are here to learn patience, your patience will be tried and tested. To learn tolerance, you will be placed in compromising situations with others who have different belief systems. Seek to know your purpose, set your goals for accomplishment and work with all your might. "The hand of the diligent makes rich." (Prov. 10:4)

Put your faith in the Almighty first, then in people. Do not worry about what others might think of you or your talents. Transcend others' criticism and ask the great Master to reveal your mission, and He will provide a clear answer. "For I know the plans I have for you, 'says the Lord,' plans of peace, to give you a future and a hope." (Jer. 29:11)

You will find that your purpose on your daily walk is to try to be conscious of your thoughts, intentions, and emotions and to learn from each moment. Think in terms of touching another daily in some simple way—with a smile, a kind deed or an inspiring word. Whatever your position in life, these good works can be achieved. Respect your own gifts and talents, and use them wisely for the glory of the Creator.

Prayer for Soul Purpose

*You created us, Father, in Your infinite wisdom
for a special purpose this lifetime. Each one of us
has unique talents, skills, and gifts that we can
share with others. Help us to know what our true
soul purpose is so that we can serve You better
and bring joy to humanity. We honor and revere
You and praise Your wondrous creations. Guide
and influence us to choose the perfect career path
in which we can fulfill our soul's mission. We are
all equal in Your eyes, and yet each one of us has
different qualities. Place confidence in the core of
our being so that we can move forward through
adversity and challenge. And at the end of each
working day, let us come to You in gratitude,
with thankfulness in our hearts.*

Amen.

— CHAPTER 20 —

❦

Prayer

P*rayer* is a powerful form of energetic thought which reverently reaches out to God in communion and oneness. It can be said anytime, anywhere. Jesus relished His time alone and retreated to the mountains to pray. "Evening and morning and at noon will I pray, and cry aloud, and He will hear my voice." (Ps. 55:17) Prayer can be given as an informal expression of praise or as a request for an urgent need. Commune with God in expectation. Find Him in nature and in the sights and sounds of the changing seasons. Come to Him with an attitude of gratitude and a feeling of a close, intimate relationship. He will always meet your needs. "Continue earnestly in prayer, being vigilant in it with thanksgiving." (Col. 4:2)

The practice of prayer is a source of divine communication which gives honor to a glorious Higher Power of love, light, and wisdom. Prayer renews faith and banishes anxiety. "Be anxious for nothing, but in everything by prayer, with thanksgiving, let your requests be made known to God; and the peace of God which surpasses all understanding, will guard your hearts and minds through Christ Jesus." (Phil. 4:6-7)

Count your blessings daily and implore God to help those who are underprivileged and abused. Do not despair if it seems your prayers are not answered immediately. Be patient, for no prayer goes unheard or unanswered. God's thoughts and timing may not be your timing, as your human ways are not necessarily God's ways. "'For My thoughts *are* not your thoughts, nor *are* your ways My ways,' says the Lord. 'For as the heavens are higher than the earth, so are My ways higher than your ways, and My thoughts than your thoughts.'" (Is. 55:8-9)

A simple childlike prayer said in true sincerity can be more powerful than the recitation of prayers done half-heartedly. Always make prayer a daily practice to obtain courage and inner peace. "Take the helmet of salvation, and the sword of the Spirit, which is the word of God; praying always with all prayer and supplication in the Spirit . . ." (Eph. 6:17-18).

It is advantageous for soul growth, to reach out in prayer, but also to go within yourself through meditation. Many answers come in the quiet moments of life. Engaging in the practice of meditation will keep your mind open and emotions calm.

Prayer

Heavenly Father, we ask that You hear and answer our requests. We believe that no prayer goes unheard or unanswered. There is power in communing with You. Let us reach up to You with open arms and hearts. Keep our prayers simple and honest, knowing that in You, we place our trust. Lead us to a place where we can transcend the cares of this world. In gratitude we praise Your holy name. We pray that You will bestow grace upon us and show us Your favor. Let us look beyond earth's shadows to the heavenly joy that awaits us. We pray for world peace, for the ill, for the poor, and for the distressed. We pray for the lost and the underprivileged. We thank You for all that You have given to us, and we honor Your mighty gifts and blessings. Let us stay close to Your word as we travel along life's path, in Christ's name,

Amen.

— CHAPTER 21 —

❧

Meditation

Meditation is beneficial, as are prayers, to enable the feeling of connection with the Master. It brings enlightenment, through clarity of listening, while going within. Since prayer fulfills your needs by extending gratitude and communication to the Creator, it is good to practice both.

It is wise to take an accounting of your life daily. In the morning, arise early and retreat to a quiet spot. Think about the positive aspects of your life and how God has provided for you—your mind, body, soul and your very breath. Have confidence to know that what inspires your heart and motivates your being (for the good) is from the Source.

You can tap into universal knowledge by stilling your mind and calming your thought processes. This experience is referred to as meditation. The phrase, "Be still and know that I *am* God" (Ps. 46:10) means just that. This conscious resting must be done when you are awake for it has nothing to do with sleep. When you sleep, you are in an altered state where your soul can commune with the heavenly realms. What is referred to here is simply practicing "peace, be still," to encourage stopping amid a chaotic world and focusing within.

When all thoughts leave your mind, and you concentrate on one thing—a mountain landscape, a tranquil seascape, or a positive word like love—you are resting in the moment. Some people see images in their mind or feel impressions, while others hear insights. "Your ears shall hear a word behind you, saying, 'This *is* the way, walk in it . . .'" (Is. 30:21) People have thousands of thoughts every day that can intrude on their well-being. Chronic negative thinking can produce stress, high blood pressure, and illness. Therefore, it is good to meditate for at least thirty minutes each day. The heart rate and pulse slow down, and a calm inner peace is achieved. Meditation is a discipline that helps you to relax, while many revelations will unfold for your highest good. ". . . whatever things are true, whatever things are noble, whatever things are just, whatever things are pure, whatever things are lovely, whatever things are of good report, if *there is* any virtue, if *there is* anything praiseworthy—meditate on these things." (Phil. 4:8)

Meditation is not just an Eastern philosophy, but is valuable for everyone; it brings you closer to the heartbeat of God, enabling deeper spiritual understanding. To obtain true peace (which is always found within), the body, mind, and spirit must be still and at rest. In this age it is most vital for everyone to find their own connection to universal wisdom through their thought-forms. "And do not be conformed to this world, but be transformed by the renewing of your mind . . ." (Rom. 12:2)

Try this positive meditation:

Close your eyes and take eight slow, deep breaths. Visualize a clear, pristine lake that has a mirrored surface. Look deep into the water to see what is underneath and beyond. In your mind, observe and study your own reflection. Let light surround your face and notice the sun sparkling on the surface of the water. Remove every thought and focus on your image. Send love to your own reflection in the water. Do this for several minutes. Now slowly bring your consciousness back into your body. You have now cleared all negative thoughts away and will be able to see the world with greater clarity.

To feel well balanced, another beneficial exercise is to start by deep breathing, then close your eyes and in your mind, envision yourself suspended in a bubble of your favorite color. Feel the color pulsing through your body and revitalizing each cell. Colors can affect moods and the energy patterns around you. Pink light represents unconditional love, while purple denotes intuition and alignment with the Higher Power. Bright blue brings calm and protection; golden yellow infuses the energy of mental clarity. Green is the hue of nature, healing, and emotional cleansing. It is good to imagine one of these colors surrounding your body to clear your energy field. If you are drawn to visualize warmer colors such as yellow, orange, and red, then you need the power of these colors at that moment.

True peace must come from within, from the core of self. So be encouraged to stop, reflect, and meditate daily. "My mouth shall speak wisdom, and the meditation of my heart *shall* give understanding." (Ps. 49:3)

Prayer for Meditation

Dear God, give us tranquility to enable us to still our minds and hearts to hear Your voice. Whether we sit in silence to listen for spiritual insights or find answers on a peaceful nature walk, may we feel Your loving presence with us. Let us take time from this busy world to stop and reflect on all our blessings. Let us find enlightenment by going within and from this place of peace to learn greater understanding and divine wisdom.

Amen

CHAPTER 22

✦

Health and Healing

Your physical body is a temple that houses your eternal spirit. "Do you not know that your body is the temple of the Holy Spirit *who* is in you, whom you have from God . . .?" (1 Cor 6:19)

Pace yourself in the workplace, for overworking produces stress, and stress produces illness. Your life journey should be enjoyed, but overindulgence in food, drink, drugs or promiscuity is unwise. Some people submerge hurts through self-abuse. This behavior is caused by low self-esteem and trust issues. Forgive those who have hurt you and move on.

Cherish and nurture your body with good nutrition. Eat more raw foods such as seasonal fruits, vegetables, and greens. In the book of Genesis God gave Adam and Eve permission to eat freely from the plant foods. Fresh fish is an excellent source of protein and omega 3 fish oil will sooth internal organs. "These you may eat of all that *are* in the water; whatever in the water has fins and scales, whether in the seas or in the rivers—that you may eat." (Lev. 11:9) Lean beef, lamb, bison, and deer are mentioned in the *Old Testament* and are also excellent sources of protein." Among the animals, whatever divides the hoof, having cloven hooves *and* chewing the cud—that you may eat." (Lev 11:3) Almonds and almond oil also provide protein and are good for the system. Olive oil lubricates the intestines and used topically will soften the skin. Vitamin B-100 complex energizes and de-stresses the immune system, and aids in blood circulation. Red wine in moderation improves the heart rate and oxygenates the bloodstream. Each day, throughout the year, try to get some sun on your face and forearms. This will alleviate depression and help with vitamin D production.

Get adequate rest and drink copious amounts of purified or distilled water, which flushes toxins from the body. Take walks in nature, stretch, exercise, pray and meditate. Therapeutic massage relaxes the muscles of the body. Laughter releases chemical endorphins and creates a feeling of well-being.

Make a conscious effort to balance your mind, body, and spirit. Humans have the capacity, with God's will, to heal themselves through faith. Disease comes from variable factors; stress, abuse in childhood, fragmented relationships, and negative emotions that stem from fear. Thoughts are powerful transmitters, and therefore it's advantageous to stay in a positive mood.

If you can create illness in the body through negativity, then you can heal your body by recognizing the source of the negativity and releasing it. Many times, pain and disease will be in certain parts of the body to get our attention. Back pain denotes heavy responsibility and burdens that are being carried. Leg cramps or edema in the lower extremities could indicate the inability to make a change or move forward for self-growth. When you are ill, realize what part of your body is affected and try to understand the negative thought or event that has caused it. Then release the negativity and visualize the area surrounded with healing white light. Rebuke the illness to go, claim a miracle and thank God for your healing now! "Beloved, I pray you may prosper in all things and be in health, just as your soul prospers." (3 John 2)

Still, even the greatest healers may have difficulty healing themselves. It is much easier to have a trusted facilitator to help us with the healing process. This may be a doctor, spiritual healer, or some other practitioner you believe in. Though Jesus was an extraordinary healer, He was only the facilitator for us. "God anointed Jesus of Nazareth with the Holy Spirit and with power, who went about doing good and healing all those who were oppressed . . ." (Acts 10:38)

Faith is important for healing. If you believe that the facilitator who is doing the healing can help you, then you will be healed. Christ is within every man, woman, and child, so, you are heirs to healing yourselves, . . . and you can. Prayer releases faith with positive thought forms and expedites miracles. "Confess *your* trespasses to one another, and pray for one another, that you may be healed. The effective, fervent prayer of a righteous man avails much." (Jas. 5:16) Humanity is part of the Godhead, and you are co-creators with the Source. Therefore, you can heal yourself if the will and intent are there.

When you are in the flow of God's love, then healing occurs. Many lightworkers who are now on earth are wonderful healers. But realize that they are just the facilitators for the healing, depending upon the belief system of the recipient. Forgiveness is also synonymous with healing.

The following exercise will bring you closer to total well-being:

Go back over your life (in your mind) and start with the earliest memory of trauma. Forgive the person who inflicted it. If you have abused yourself, then forgive yourself. Look at your inner child and love him or her unconditionally.

Be aware that miracles exist and give God the glory. Disease is an imbalance between the mind, body, and spirit. All areas must be balanced for perfect health and alignment. If you are mindful that healing starts within yourself and with *faith*, you simply say, "Lord, heal by your touch," and you will be healed. "For I will restore health to you and heal you of your wounds . . ." (Jer. 30:17) Through faith, you are aligning your inner potential with God's love, and by doing so, healing miracles will occur.

Prayer for Health and Healing

*Dear Lord, we believe You want us to prosper
and be in perfect health, as our souls prosper.
Give us guidance to nourish our bodies and to
give sustenance to these temples in which our
souls are housed. Let us only eat food and drink
beverages that are for our highest good. Give
us discernment to know what forms of exercise
we should pursue, and what lifestyle suits our
earthly mission. If we are ill, let us know we
can be healed through faith and belief in Your
power. Restore healing in our minds, bodies,
and spirits. We ask this in the name of the
great healer, Jesus.*

Amen.

❧

CHAPTER 23

Miracles

Miracles are supernatural events, gifts of mercy, and beloved favor from the Higher Power. "Every good gift and every perfect gift is from above, and comes down from the Father of lights . . ." (Jas. 1:17). Some people think that there are standard ingredients that create miracles. Miracles happen, not by chance, nor by cause and effect, but through the love and divine grace of God. "Now God worked unusual miracles . . ." (Acts 19:11)

As was mentioned, if a healer is moved with compassion to help an ill person, and if that diseased person has faith to believe in healing, then a miracle may transpire. Faith puts miracles into motion! The *working of miracles* is one of the nine gifts of the Holy Spirit. (Reference 1 Cor. 12:10) The scope of miracles is vast and occurs daily in nature and in our own lives. They may be subtle—like the changing of the seasons—yet even though we don't always recognize them, they still exist. Miracles can range from simple manifestations which come into being, to life-changing circumstances—a child who is saved from an accident, rain showers during drought, an incurable disease that is healed, an estranged family relationship that is restored, addictions being released, a lost pet that is found, the birth of a baby and so on.

These events are orchestrated through God's unmerited assistance. The Lord knows all, has created all that exists and dwells within all living things. Positive prayers, trusting in God, and unshakable belief are the catalysts that initiate them.

Miracles are in the eye of the beholder! As the great Einstein said, "There are two ways to live your life. One is as though nothing is a miracle. The other is as though everything is." Miracles are for the regeneration of humanity and the showering of blessings. "Surely blessings, I will bless you and multiplying I will multiply you." (Heb. 6:14).

Be encouraged to pray, commune within, meditate, and contemplate God's divinity. From within, you will be given the understanding and wisdom the world cannot give you . . . and there you will find peace and the true meaning of miracles.

Prayer for Miracles

*Father, we believe in Your grace and in miracles!
Let us perceive all of life as a miracle and
acknowledge miracles daily. We understand they
are gifts of mercy and love from You, and we
thank You for them. You created all through the
miracle of love, so we, in turn, will try to love
one another, as You love us. We praise and honor
Your mighty name.*

Amen.

About the Author

M ichele A. Livingston is an internationally known visionary, spiritual counselor, gifted artist, and interfaith minister. With a Master's Degree in art education, she taught art in public schools and later displayed her work in her own art gallery. For the last thirty years Michele has brought comfort, closure, and peace to those seeking answers about heaven with her spiritual counseling. Michele has hosted her own radio show, had her own TV show, has made numerous guest appearances on national programs, and currently does video podcasts.

As a healer and counselor, she continues to bring spiritual messages and soul healing guidance to people throughout the world as she assists them in taking the next step in love to become closer to the Creator.

Michele is available for radio and TV interviews, seminars, group sessions, phone, and in-person consultations. For more information on Michele Livingston please visit her website at www.MicheleLivingston.com or call (717) 737-3888.

www.ingramcontent.com/pod-product-compliance
Lightning Source LLC
Chambersburg PA
CBHW030515100426

42813CB00001B/51

* 9 7 8 1 6 2 0 0 6 2 6 0 9 *